DRIVER TUNE-UP

Henry
Ramirez

SAFETY

ISBN 978-1-79485-654-7

10 9 8 7 6 5 4 3 2 1

I dedicate this book to my grandchildren, their grandchildren and all their friends.

Contents

Introduction

The purpose of this book is to help drivers avoid collisions.

During the years when I was a California Highway Patrol officer, I investigated a lot of wrecks. But at collision scenes, I had a limited ability to educate the drivers who were considered at fault.

Now, I'd like to persuade every driver to evaluate their own driving history and performance.

Ask yourself: "How good is my driving?"

It is unfortunate that our society accepts the notion that traffic collisions will occur. There is a mindset that we should accept traffic collisions, because they are inevitable.

All traffic collisions could be avoided if every person behind the wheel were to make safe driving a priority, and concentrate on not being part of a problem that has been neglected too long.

We strive to be good drivers. We are hopeful, too, that our loved ones don't imitate the poor driving examples that contribute to collision statistics. I hope that a periodic driver tune-up will improve your driving performance. The key to defensive driving is to *stay focused*.

Take a look at the following statements. If any of them apply, then this book is intended for you.

1. You feel that your driving performance has gravely deteriorated.
2. You want to fine-tune your performance to gain confidence.
3. You question your ability to handle your driving responsibilities.
4. You have been involved in several traffic collisions, or have experienced close calls.
5. You are the parent of a teenager, responsible for your daughter or son's behind-the-wheel training.
6. You're a teenager or an adult learning to drive for the first time.
7. You are a nanny responsible for transporting children.
8. You are a senior driver who is required to be retested by the Department of Motor Vehicles or Traffic Safety office.
9. You are a driving instructor, and want a few tips to improve your teaching skills.
10. You work for a ride-hailing company and would like to improve your performance. (In my experience, every hailing-company driver I've ridden with has committed at least one critical driving error).

With all this said, please keep in mind that this book contains a collection of *suggestions*. In my experience as a driving instructor, these concepts have proven very helpful in restructuring poor habits and increasing confidence. Remember that every person learns at their own pace. Not all suggestions will benefit everyone.

About the Author

Henry Ramirez worked for the California Highway Patrol for twenty-five years. After starting as a traffic officer, and working both in a patrol car and on a motorcycle, he was promoted to state traffic sergeant and state traffic lieutenant. He holds the lifetime Standard Designated Teaching Credential in Public Safety and Accident Prevention, including driver education and driver training. He is a graduate of California State University Los Angeles with a Bachelor of Police Science and Administration degree.

While performing his CHP responsibilities, Henry taught driver education, behind-the-wheel training, traffic school and special courses for DUI first offenders.

As the former owner of Bay Area Driving School, based in Hayward, California, Henry served as the driving analyst. For forty years, he specialized in helping students with special needs. Some of his students have included individuals with autism or developmental disabilities; those with phobias (fear of freeway driving, bridges, and tunnels); people on the verge of losing their job due to poor driving; and senior citizens wanting to maintain their driving privileges.

Acknowledgments

I wish to offer my heartfelt thanks to my family for their deep love and continual support, which provides the basis for everything I do. Thanks also to my former students who encouraged me to write this book, to share this information with everyone who is willing to make a difference in traffic safety. Thanks to the dedicated employees of Bay Area Driving School. Thanks to all traffic enforcement officers who are dedicated to keeping our highways safe. Thanks to the members of the Driving School Association of California and the Driving School Association of the Americas for their commitment in developing safe drivers in our country. And finally, thanks to my editors, Amelia Sue Marshall and Jodi Compton, who insisted on perfection and brought out the best I had to offer.

ONE

The Initial Driving Experience

Let's go back a few years, to the time when you seriously made up your mind that you wanted to drive. Do you remember other people telling you that driving was easy? Perhaps someone told you that driving was like learning to walk, or riding a bicycle. When you have four wheels, you don't have to worry about balance, as you would with riding a motorcycle or bicycle.

The main point of this well-meaning advice was that once you mastered the task of learning to drive a car, you would never forget it.

The responsibilities required for driving and for riding a bicycle are similar. A bicyclist has to maintain balance and control of his or her bicycle at all times, obey the traffic laws, avoid pedestrians or animals that might stray into the bike lane, and ride *very* defensively.

Pedestrians and bicyclists today are very vulnerable, especially those who have their eyes and attention focused on their phones while they are walking near traffic, or riding in it. When people ignore the responsibility to be aware of their own safety, it is you - the driver - who will need to handle potential conflicts. Remember, when it is metal versus flesh, there is no contest!

Is your teenager a prospective driver?

First, ask yourself the most important question: Is this

young person mature enough to handle the responsibilities of safely operating a motor vehicle?

In more detail, this means, is he or she ready to *always* maintain control of the car and obey the rules of the road? Can he or she maintain a calm and courteous attitude? Handle unexpected traffic situations by making quick, sound, rational decisions?

Young people in their high school years are usually gifted with good cognitive and motor skills – their vision, reaction time, and hearing set the stage for them to become good drivers. And, certainly, most teenagers welcome the challenge of learning to drive.

Driving instructors know that teenagers are easier to teach than older people. High school students have been waiting patiently for this moment in life; they want to take this giant step towards adulthood. At this age, too, they are less fearful.

Personally, I prefer to start fresh with someone who has never driven a motor vehicle. With a brand-new driver, it is possible to incorporate good techniques from the outset. I won't need to spend a lot of time correcting bad habits they picked up from their parents or friends.

Teenagers need to focus on gaining driving experience, maintaining a mature attitude and making good decisions.

Parents should be mindful of their own behavior when driving, and the impressions those behaviors make on their youngsters.

Parents should also remember to stay involved, and to monitor their teens' driving skill, even well after they get their license.

Some of today's beginners think that driving a car is like driving a Go-Cart or playing video games. They jerk the steering wheel abruptly, as if it were a joystick. During video games, participants hit objects and crash; then the imaginary vehicle reassembles and the game continues. The real world does not work like that!

Teenagers need to learn to do everything possible to avoid traffic collisions. They need to remember that the less you move the steering wheel, the straighter the vehicle will travel. Beginners often have the mistaken impression that they have to be active in order to maintain proper alignment on the road. Driving responsibilities require multitasking. All at the same time, you must:

1. Control your vehicle;
2. Obey the traffic laws; and
3. Be able to make good decisions when confronted with hazardous situations, including (and especially) errant drivers of other vehicles.

To be safe drivers, we all need to continuously tune up our driving performance, avoid picking up bad habits, and strive to drive defensively. In 2015, according to the National Highway Traffic Safety Administration, 35,092 people were killed, and an estimated 2,443,000 people injured, in police-reported crashes.[1]

Do you remember when you first received your driver's license? It was exciting because you were allowed to take out a car by yourself for the first time. What a lot of us didn't understand is that perfecting our driving skill is a lifelong experience. We need to put safe driving at the top of our priorities, so that we reach our destinations safely. I truly believe that we can all contribute to keeping traffic collisions down to a very minimum if we evaluate our driving performance on a daily basis.

---

1   National Highway Traffic Safety Administration, "Traffic Safety Facts," October 2017, https://crashstats.nhtsa.dot.gov/Api/Public/ViewPublication/812376 (accessed 6/3/2019).

TWO

Understanding the Traffic Collision Problem.

(It Is Not OK to Crash)

(Not a desirable transportation option.)

I entered the California Highway Patrol academy in May 1969. During my traffic collision investigation training, I learned that the term "traffic accident" was a misnomer. The correct term was "traffic collision." This stuck in my mind.

The term "accident" implies too much chance and too little culpability. The majority of investigators would agree that the main factor in the majority of crashes was *driver error* - someone disobeyed a traffic law. The National Highway Traffic Safety Administration states that "The critical reason, which is the last event in the crash causal chain, was assigned to the driver in 94 percent (±2.2%)†

of the crashes."[2] A review of most collision reports will clearly direct your attention to the section called "Primary Collision Factors."

Some of the most common factors are:

- Unsafe speed
- Unsafe lane change
- Unsafe turning movement
- Failure to stop for a stop sign or signal
- Failure to yield the right of way
- Following too closely
- Driving on the wrong side of the road
- Driving under the influence of alcohol and/or drugs

There is a mindset that we should accept traffic collisions, because they are inevitable. Some motorists say, "I was at the wrong place at the wrong time." Others say, "life just happens" or "it wasn't my fault." However, allowing our mind to focus on irrelevant thoughts or distractions makes us more vulnerable.

Any time someone waves at you with one finger (flips you off), yells at you, or blasts their horn, this should serve as a wake-up call. Annoying as these experiences can be,

------

2   US Department of Transportation: National Highway Traffic Safety Administration, "Traffic Safety Facts: Critical Reasons for Crashes Investigated in the National Motor Vehicle Crash Causation Survey," February 2015. https://crashstats.nhtsa.dot.gov/Api/Public/ViewPublication/812115 (accessed 6/3/2019).

they are clues that others are not happy with your driving. This is the time to ask yourself, "Is there something I am doing wrong?"

I envision every traffic situation as a puzzle. Everyone in the situation is part of the puzzle. If a piece is defective (an errant driver), the picture will likely create conflict.

It is our responsibility to eliminate traffic collisions. Do you personally know of a case where a collision has caused unnecessary injury, or property damage … or even a fatality?

THREE

How Can We Rectify the Traffic Collision Problem?

As we are driving, we are interacting with other members of our community. Our first step should be to see them as family members, neighbors, and innocent bystanders. For this reason, we have a moral obligation to drive safely and courteously.

For example, when you observe a sticker on a car stating, "Baby on Board," the driver is trying to convey the idea that they are traveling with the most precious little person in their life.

I like to take it a step further. How about "Mom/Dad on Board?" "Sister/Brother on Board?" "Priest/Pastor/Rabbi on Board?" Or how about just "Human on Board?"

Our behavior behind the wheel affects everyone. We must believe that we can make a difference - by not being part of the collision problem.

With *Driver Tune-Up*, I hope that you will evaluate your own driving performance. I hope that you will resolve to improve your driving skills, will learn to avoid making the same mistake twice, and will strive to be a defensive driver.

Have you ever heard the old saying: "One way to stay fresh is to never get stale?"

To be a safe driver, it is essential to discipline one's mind. Our thoughts are sometimes restless and difficult to control. Allowing our mind to focus on irrelevant subjects or distractions will make us more vulnerable when driving in traffic.

To be a safe driver, it is essential to consciously unplug ourselves from the technology that invades our lives. While paying attention to a cell phone, navigation device, or other screen, we cannot focus on maintaining complete control of our driving, obeying traffic laws, and handling any situation that comes up.

The root of the problem lies in our priorities behind the wheel. For too many drivers, traffic safety does not rank high enough.

To be a safe driver, it is important to establish the right mindset. When we are behind the wheel, we need to focus on making our driving responsibilities our *number-one priority*. While we are in motion, we must commit our undivided attention to these responsibilities. We must filter out passenger conversation, children's antics, radio programs, and music. There is no room for error. One critical driving error could be your last.

FOUR

Respecting and Obeying Traffic Laws

Traffic regulations are necessary. How else can we help motorists make proper decisions, maintain order and safety on our roadways, and protect human life?

Without traffic laws, motorists would not know who has the right-of-way, what speed is safe, and what to do when approaching a hazard.

As a CHP traffic officer, one of my primary responsibilities was to enforce the laws. I always felt that one of the most important attributes of an officer was to have good discretion.

I got to meet many interesting motorists, and I tried to treat them in the manner that I would like to be treated if our situations were reversed. Still, I usually had my mind made up as to what enforcement action I was going to take before making my initial contact with the violator.

During traffic stops, motorists will benefit if they are courteous to the traffic officer.

Sometimes, a motorist is only given a verbal warning. If this happens to you, the best course of action is to thank the officer and leave. On the other hand, if you are impolite, argumentative and disrespectful, there is nothing to preclude the officer from changing his or her mind and issuing you a citation.

Once, I stopped a young lady who had been driving erratically. When she opened her window, I could see that she had tears in her eyes. She said that she was distraught because her mother had passed away. Next to her, I could see a funeral announcement confirming her loss. Although my initial decision had been to issue her a citation, I waited until she gained her composure, gave her a verbal warning, and let her go home.

My youngest son has followed my career path. He, too, serves as a State Traffic Officer with the California Highway Patrol. He and his colleagues strive to keep our highways safe 24/7, by addressing the violations that endanger the public. Traffic officers have a dangerous job. When they stop a driver, they never know who they are confronting. They must always use extreme caution. I pray for them every day, that they complete their duties and return safely to their families.

FIVE

Why Do People Violate Traffic Laws?

There are many reasons why people break traffic laws.

One reason is *lack of education*.

Knowledge of the rules of the road is the foundation of safe and competent driving. Understanding right-of-way rules is essential for avoiding collisions. You would be surprised to learn how many people do not know these basic traffic rules. These drivers are potential hazards to other drivers.

Many times, when I was investigating collisions, the involved parties would come up to me and ask, "Who was at fault?" The fact that they had to ask this question told me that these drivers did not learn, until after the fact, what action was required of them to avoid conflict with other motorists.

The Driver Handbook provided by the Department of Motor Vehicles (or Department of Safety, in some states) covers only the basic information necessary for obtaining a driver's license. For a much better understanding of traffic laws, I recommend an in-person classroom experience, rather than an online program. Despite the convenience of the computer-based classes offered for students with busy schedules, when it comes to navigating the life-and-death situations drivers encounter, there is no substitute for social learning.

Students can learn more in the classroom setting. They have the opportunity to consult with a professional instructor to clarify any misunderstandings. In California, teenagers who apply to get their driver's license at the age of 16 must complete 30 hours of driver education and a minimum of six hours of behind-the-wheel training.

I think that it is unfortunate that many teenagers now wait until they are 18 years of age to apply for their driver instruction permit, in order to bypass the driver education and driver training requirements. Ultimately, it's a disservice to them not to get proper education before they get behind the wheel.

Sometimes, when I am supposed to be providing behind-the-wheel training, I find that I am teaching material that should have been covered in classroom driver education. Once the student is with me in the car, we need to focus on operating the vehicle. Of course, for people of all ages, driver education is an ongoing learning process.

We drivers learn from our professional instructor, our parents, other motorists' performance and our personal experience.

Let's return to my experiences where motorists have asked me, "What did I do, Officer?" It is evident that these individuals are learning from their mistakes.

Other reasons people break traffic laws include poor judgment, indecisiveness, distractions, or being late for an appointment. By having the self-discipline to allow ten extra minutes in your schedule, you will find that you save yourself a lot of anxiety.

Then there are the violators who have a disregard for authority and traffic regulations. Some have actually informed me that they always speed or go through posted stop signs. We can only hope that the fine they pay after getting caught will make up for all the times they got away with it. To these errant drivers, breaking the law is a game. They are the players, and the traffic officers are the referees. What they do not take into account is that they jeopardize the safety of innocent drivers, cyclists and pedestrians as well as their own. Driving is not a game.

When you observe a motorist intentionally violating traffic laws, it is obvious that he or she has a disregard for other community members. Their behavior is a reflection of their personality. While you can certainly report dangerous drivers if you wish, do not try to confront them. Remember, you don't know who you are dealing with. Road-rage reactions can be devastating.

When we drive responsibly, safety prevails; all motorists win, because we will arrive at our destinations safely.

SIX

Distractions Must Be Eliminated

According to the National Highway Traffic Safety Administration, "Using a cell phone while driving creates enormous
potential for deaths and injuries on U.S. roads. In 2017
alone, 3,166 people were killed in motor vehicle crashes
involving distracted drivers."[3]

Talking on the mobile phone is a catalyst of fatal events.
There is no safe way to talk on a phone while driving. Even
adding a hands-free device, earphone, speaker connection
or elaborate dashboard communication system isn't an ideal
fix; even though the driver's hands are free, the mind is still
distracted.

Certainly, mobile phones have now become an essential
part of life for most people. They help us stay connected and
increase our productivity. Smartphones have proven deadly
on the roads, however. It is unwise to use smartphones in a
manner that puts everyone on the road at risk.

Some Effective Ways to Eliminate Distracted Driving

- Use a free automated response application that lets
  callers know that you're driving and can't take their
  call.
- Vehicles can be outfitted with a "Do Not Disturb"
  feature. This allows you to unplug from calls and texts

------

3   National Highway Traffic Safety Administration, "Distracted Driving," April, 2019.
    https://www.nhtsa.gov/risky-driving/distracted-driving (accessed 6/3/2019).

while behind the wheel.

- Use shared calendars to block the times when you'll be driving. This alerts anyone else connected to your calendar when you are out of touch.
- When you sit down behind the wheel, place your phone out of reach; for example, you could put it on the back seat.
- If you know it will be necessary to take an incoming call, let it go to voice mail. Find a safe place to pull over and then return the call.
- Plan your route ahead of time to avoid becoming disoriented and losing focus.
- When you are using a navigation device, plug in the coordinates of your destination *before* you step on the accelerator. Preview all of the directions, so that you're prepared. Always pay attention to the audio – not the visual screen - as you are cruising down the road.
- All technology will be a distraction to drivers, some of the time; this includes everything from in-car telematics to digital devices. The technology we use is more powerful and complicated than ever before.
- Properly restrain dogs while the vehicle is moving. Depending on the size of the dog and the type of vehicle, use a safety–certified, crash-tested crate or any of a number of products available to comfortably restrain animals in the back seat or hatchback area. (*Never* close an animal in a sealed trunk.) As with small children, don't let a dog ride up in the front, because he or she could be injured or killed in a crash

by the deploying airbag. *Never* be foolish enough to let your pooch, however tiny and lovable, ride on your lap while driving.

The Ultimate Goal

Remember that the driver should only have one job: to drive, staying focused on the road. Anything that shifts attention away from the road is a distraction and should be used when the gearshift is in "Park."

SEVEN

How Insurance Companies Can Help

Insurance companies should be more proactive in eliminating traffic collisions, rather than trying to recruit new customers with feel-good slogans like "Accident Forgiveness." This phrase gives the impression that we expect collisions to occur, and that this company will insure you without penalizing you.

Insurance companies could use their marketing to correct other misconceptions, too. For example, they should not convey the false impression that because we are human, we are prone to mistakes: For instance, opening the car door in traffic, or backing into the garage while forgetting that the bicycle is on the rack on top of the car.

On the other hand, some insurance companies reward exemplary driving. One good example of this is companies that issue "Safe Driving Bonus Checks" or insurance discounts.

Some insurance companies are using palm-sized devices, often called "tattletales," that consumers can voluntarily install. This gadget connects into a car's on-board diagnostic port to track driving parameters such as mileage, speed, and braking intensity, mapped to time of day. These companies challenge their customers to provide this accurate data to prove that they present a lower risk of collision. In return, the drivers pay lower insurance rates.

Another device is called "Snapshot." It is a plug-in device

that tracks the time of day and records how often the driver slams on the brakes. This data calculates the number of miles a customer drives, as well.

While these types of devices could assist insurance companies in identifying drivers who have poor habits and performance, I feel that more emphasis should be directed toward *motivating* drivers to improve. Insurance customers are more likely to strive to be collision-free if they receive lower rates each year they succeed at this.

Here's an anecdote that illustrates that idea: Once, many years ago, our driving school had an instructor who felt that it was OK to crash a car each year! This instructor rationalized that his job was dangerous; our daily exposure to traffic increased our chances of being involved in collisions.

Around that time, we set up a bonus program. Instructors who completed a year with no preventable traffic collisions received a bonus reward. Are you surprised to learn that the instructor in question went on to complete numerous consecutive collision-free years? He looked forward to receiving the bonus reward during the Christmas holidays.

EIGHT

Proper Attitude and Mindset When Operating a Motor Vehicle

We drivers need to filter out distractions.

For safe driving, our mindset must focus on always maintaining control of our driving performance, obeying all traffic laws and handling any situation we confront.

Put the darn phone down!

It only takes one lapse of awareness, when a driver is distracted by a phone call, to cause injury, loss of income, societal medical costs, and perhaps significant disability and death. It's not worth it.

Forming Good Driving Habits

One key to improving your driving performance is to practice long enough that good procedures become a habit. It takes about three weeks to instill a new habit. [4]

Try this idea: Challenge yourself to try an improved driving practice for three weeks. For example, instead of rolling through stop signs, force yourself to come to a complete stop and count, "One-Two-Three" before proceeding.

If you stick with the change long enough, you'll form a habit that becomes second nature. You won't even have to

---

4   Charles Duhigg, "The Power of Habit," 2012. Random House Trade Paperbacks.

think about the improvement.

When you drive a car, you are like the director of a movie, controlling every movement of the actors, orchestrating the conflicts that arise. You need to stay alert. It is your job to eliminate anything that will degrade the quality of the picture. The more we retain control of ourselves and our vehicle, the less likely it is that another, errant driver will determine the outcome of a situation.

Strive to extend courtesy to others without placing yourself in a vulnerable position. Courtesy is contagious. Many times, when you extend courtesy to motorists, they are prone to passing it on to others. Also, when courtesy is extended to you, acknowledge it with a simple hand wave.

NINE

Critical Driving Errors that Need Serious Consideration

Speed Control

Once, when I was ten years old, my father took me on the train to visit my grandmother in Mexico.

When the train reached its cruising speed, I noticed the telephone poles we were passing resembled toothpicks as we zipped by. As the train approached each designated stop, the engineer reduced speed. Then, the telephone poles appeared to pass in slow motion.

I made an observation: the slower we travelled, the more I observed pedestrians, the landscape and what was happening outside my window.

The same concept applies to driving a vehicle at higher speeds. When a car is going too fast, it not only affects visibility, the speed makes it difficult for the driver to maneuver on turns and when stopping.

Let me share a true story: Some high school students had nothing to do on a very foggy Saturday night. They decided to play follow-the-leader on a winding, narrow road.

I was supervising the CHP graveyard shift when the call came in: it was a collision involving multiple vehicles, with unknown details.

When I arrived at the scene, I noticed that a vehicle had run off the road. The next four vehicles each rear-ended the vehicle ahead of them. Tow trucks were dispatched to the scene for the disabled vehicles. The investigating officer took statements of the drivers and passengers. We determined that the leading vehicle was traveling too fast for the foggy condition, lost control and ran off the road.

Furthermore, *all* the drivers were traveling too fast for the foggy conditions, because the next four teenage drivers were following too closely.

Can you imagine the looks on the parents' faces when they read the report and recognized the names of the other parties involved?

When you try to challenge the physical limitation of a vehicle or a road, most of the time you will lose. Not only are you placing your life in harm's way, you are also jeopardizing the safety of your passengers and innocent motorists.

Worst are the drivers who are confronted with unexpected events or errant drivers while they are exceeding the posted speed limits.

Since the bulk of winter collisions are front-end related – caused by drivers going too fast for icy conditions and being unable to stop in time to prevent a rear-ending accident --matching your speed to the road conditions is an easy way to prevent injuries and fatalities. It is also an easy way to avoid costly trips to the body shop.

Adherence to the speed laws could reduce collisions tremendously. We rely on traffic engineers to establish speed limits that are safe for the roads. The National Highway Traffic Safety Administration reports state "There were 37,461 traffic fatalities in 2016. Among them, 10,111 (27 percent) were in crashes where at least one driver was speeding." [5]

Speeding increases the risk of getting into a crash. Not only that, but drivers and their passengers are more likely to be seriously injured or killed in higher-speed wrecks.

To maintain control of a vehicle during inclement weather, every motorist must determine the safe speed to travel.

Our roadways are not constructed like raceways, with banked curves and protective railings. Raceways don't have intersections, either!

Disobeying speed laws is the issue that lands the majority of people in traffic school.

One habit that will help you avoid speeding citations is

---

5   National Highway Traffic Safety Administration, "Traffic Safety Facts: Speeding," March, 2018. https://crashstats.nhtsa.dot.gov/Api/Public/ViewPublication/812480 (accessed 6/3/2019).

to glance at your speedometer every time you see a posted speed-limit sign. You know you are doing a good job when your speed is identical to the speed on the sign.

Remember the yellow speed-advisory sign (for example, the kind you see on sharply-curving off-ramps) is a *recommended* speed for the condition of a *dry roadway*.

For many years, the rule of thumb was to stay with the flow of traffic; however, be aware that if you travel just one mile over the speed limit, you are in violation.

In some California counties, speed laws are enforced by aircraft. If a group of vehicles is traveling at high speeds, the air crew can communicate with officers on the ground to identify and cite the entire group of violators.

Officers generally watch for the individual who is passing other vehicles and making multiple lane changes. This person stands out like a sore thumb.

To avoid the urge to speed, allow yourself ample time to reach your destination, and remind yourself to be patient.

While it may seem obvious, one of the most important things to remember about speed control is to control it with the accelerator. If you want to increase the speed, step on the accelerator; if you want to go slower, lift up on the accelerator. Only use the brake when it is necessary.

Excessive braking will require more trips the repair shop for brake pads and/or shoes replacement.

Another thing to remember: Unnecessary braking attracts traffic officers. You would be surprised how many motorists are arrested for Driving Under the Influence because their vehicle looks like a Christmas tree from behind, with lights going on and off for no reason.

Eliminate Lane-Related Traffic Collisions By Considering The Following Important Elements

Visibility

First, avoid displaying ornaments on the dashboard. These include dancing hula dolls, bobbleheads, and cultural dioramas. Remove large fuzzy dice, crystals, and memorabilia hanging on the inside mirror. Such items might add personality or aesthetic appeal, but they also prove to be a significant distraction. Decorations around the driver obstruct your crucial view of the road.

Some GPS devices can obstruct your vision and contribute to inattention.

Do you, or does anyone else who drives your car, have a state handicap placard? It is important to follow the warning printed on each tag: "Remove while driving a motor vehicle."

Also, avoid placing papers on the dashboard. Mail and personal objects should be kept elsewhere. Not only do these objects shift back and forth while the car is in motion, they reflect on the front windshield and are subtly annoying.

Visibility is something many motorists take for granted. Driving when the sun is out tends to make motorists less cautious than they might be at night. Yet the National Highway Traffic Administration has found that more traffic collisions occur during daylight hours than at night. [6]

Risk is somewhat reduced during nighttime driving, because headlights make vehicles more visible to other motorists. Also, more pedestrians are generally present during the daytime.

Though many drivers feel more comfortable during

---

[6]   National Highway Traffic Safety Administration, "NCSA Data Resource Website Fatality Analysis Reporting System (FARS) Encyclopedia, 2017. https://www-fars.nhtsa.dot.gov/Crashes/CrashesTime.aspx (accessed 6/3/2019).

daylight hours, pedestrians, bicycles and oncoming traffic are not always easy to see, especially when weather and road conditions are unfavorable. Daylight running lights ("DRLs"), are an effective way to improve visibility. DRLs make the vehicle easier to spot during daylight hours, and especially at dusk, when other motorists might have more difficulty seeing. Studies have shown that DRLs reduce multiple-vehicle daytime collisions by as much as ten percent.[7] Take advantage of your DRLs. Using them is an easy way to prevent daytime head-on and front-corner collisions. The lights make it easier to see a vehicle, particularly as it approaches from far away.

Keep headlamps clean. Plastic headlamp lenses become hazed and yellow over time from the effects of sunlight, ozone, road pollution and car-wash chemicals. Dirty and deteriorated headlamps compromise nighttime visibility.

Routinely check windshield washer fluid. Make sure there is enough fluid. During the winter and early spring months, snow and debris, such as sand or roadway salt, can accumulate on the windshield and make it difficult to see. If the reservoir is empty, but you don't have windshield-washer fluid at hand, do not use water as a replacement, as water can freeze and cause damage to the reservoir and hoses. Inspect wipers and replace the blades if needed. Old

---

7   Minnesota Department of Transportation, "Transportation Research Synthesis, Effects of 24 Hour Headlight Use on Traffic Safety," November, 2010. https://www.dot.state.mn.us/research/TRS/2011/TRS1009.pdf (accessed 6/3/2019)

or worn-out wiper blades can also negatively impact your ability to see.

Keep interior glass and mirrors clean. Interior glass can suffer from film buildup that can reduce a driver's vision. Glare is especially a problem during daylight hours when buildup can create a hazy reflection from the sun. This film can be especially thick in cars where drivers or passengers routinely smoke.

In addition to cleaning the interior glass, keep the rearview and side mirrors clean and properly adjusted, so your vision is not compromised while driving.

Drivers need to be able to see all of the views around the back of the car, especially the blind spots along both sides of the vehicle.

I have encountered new drivers that have difficulty keeping their vehicle in the center of the lane. The major contributing factors are as follows:

Your Seating Position - Make sure that your mouth is even with or above the steering wheel. Some vehicles have adjustable steering wheels with telescopic features. If your vehicle doesn't, use cushions to adjust the height. You do not want to be looking through the steering wheel. Some teenagers think it looks cool to sit low, but these lowriders' ability to see ahead is compromised.

Aiming High in Steering - Fighter pilots call it situational awareness; it means being upright, ready, and prepared for whatever comes. Avoid distractions. Scan the road ahead of the next few cars to see what's happening. Prepare an escape route at the first hint of trouble. This subject will be covered in more detail when we discuss defensive driving techniques.

Making Safe Lateral Maneuvers

Sideswiped vehicles have been involved in lateral maneuver traffic collisions.

One of the biggest problems with lane violations or lateral maneuvers is not adequately checking your blind spots. Any time you steer to the left or right, you should look over the corresponding shoulder. This practice gets easier through repetition and regularity.

Look Over Your Right Shoulder Prior To:

1. Changing lanes to the right;
2. Parking next to the right curb;
3. Positioning next to the corner to make a right turn;
4. Merging to the right.

Look Over Your Left Shoulder Prior To:

1. Changing lanes to the left;
2. Pulling away from the right curb;
3. Merging to the left;
4. Merging onto the freeway.

Suggested Tips in Changing Traffic Lanes

A competent driver can usually be identified by how he or she negotiates lane changes. In our complex highway system, we are constantly required to change lanes. The lane change should be safe, and executed with precision and with good rhythm. We should develop the habit of following the same steps each time we change lanes. If we don't, there is a good possibility that we will take shortcuts and interfere with other motorists.

There are *two essential* prerequisites before you attempt to change lanes:

- Get the car straight; and
- Maintain the same steady speed.

Recommended Steps for Changing Lanes:

Steps for Making a Lane Change to the Right:

1. Check your inside mirror. If there is no traffic approaching, signal right (push the turn signal lever upward).
2. Check your right-side mirror.
3. Look over your right shoulder, through the right rear window, to check the blind spot.
4. Quickly return your gaze forward. Pause. Take a second to process the information on what you have seen around the car.
5. When safe, glide into the right lane while maintaining the same speed.
6. Cancel the turn signal when the vehicle is entirely in the right lane.

Steps for Making a Lane Change to the Left:

1. Check your inside mirror. If there is no traffic approaching, signal left (push the turn signal lever downward).
2. Check your left side mirror.

3. Look over your left shoulder to check the blind spot.
4. Quickly return your gaze forward. Pause. Take a second to process what you've seen.
5. When safe, change into the left lane while accelerating to adjust for speed in a faster lane.
6. Cancel the turn signal when the vehicle is entirely in the left lane.

The most common errors in changing lanes:

1. Not looking adequately over the appropriate shoulder.
2. Applying the brake before changing lanes. When you slow down as you move to the adjacent lane, this allows traffic coming up from behind you to get closer; this reduces the safety of your lane change.
3. Using poor judgment in determining if a lane change can be completed without *interference*.

Parking Next to the Right Curb, or Pulling Away from the Right Curb

These maneuvers should be treated just the same way you negotiate the respective lane change.

Negotiating Turns

Speed control plays a very important role in negotiating turns. It is better to make turns too slow, rather than too fast. Any time you take a turn too fast, you are at risk of losing control of the vehicle.

When beginning turns, refrain from reaching inside the steering wheel with your palm up. Doing so limits your turning ability to about ¼ rotation of the steering wheel, rather than about ¾ rotation if grasping and controlling the wheel from outside with palm down. Proper grasping and movement of the steering wheel will assist you when confronted with a sudden dangerous situation, such as a child darting into your path.

Steering wheel hand positions: remember the hours 12, 3, 6, and 9 o'clock

Old-school driving instructors taught their students to hold their hands high on the steering wheel (10 o'clock and 2 o'clock position). Many driving experts say that this position risks traumatic injuries in a crash, thanks to the force and direction of airbags in modern cars. Holding the wheel at a lower position (9 o'clock and 3 o'clock), will protect a driver's hands and arms better. The 8 o'clock and 4 o'clock position is acceptable, in my opinion, when driving on highways or freeways.

Typical turns are 90 degrees, which are performed by moving the wheel a half circle (180 degrees).

I prefer the hand-over-hand technique for making turns.

Remember to start turns with the opposite hand. For a left turn, use your right hand to turn the wheel until that hand has gone from the 3 o'clock position to the 8 o'clock. Then move your left hand to the 9 position and your right to the 3. Hold the wheel this way until the turn is completed. Then use your left hand to turn the wheel back, until that hand goes from the 9 position to the 4. Then put your hands back in the 9 and 3 spots.

For a right turn, first use your left hand to turn the wheel from the 9 o'clock position to the 4 o'clock position. Then place your right hand at the 3 and your left hand at the 9. After the turn is completed, use the right hand to return the wheel from the 3 position to the 8 position. Then place your hands back at the initial 9 and 3 o'clock positions.

Common Errors in Making Right Turns

In making right turns, drivers' most frequent error is *not looking over their right shoulder prior to positioning next to the right curb.* We are looking for a sports car, motorcycle, or bicycle.

Aim to get as close as is practical to the curb. I interpret this distance to be a little shorter than the width of motorcycle or bicycle handlebars.

Normally, right turns are 90 degrees. Turns can be sharp, moderate or wide. The sharper the turn, the faster we move the steering wheel. The wider the turn, the slower we move the wheel.

The proper moment to begin a right turn is when the front of the car reaches the point where the curve begins. First, maneuver the car so that you hug the corner. Be sure you're at the proper speed to begin the turn. Identify how sharp the turn will be, and move the wheel accordingly.

Coordinating the use of the brake and gas pedal is very important for skillful turning. At the point when you are just past the middle of the turn, start returning the wheel to its straight-forward position.

In most cases, you will need to complete the right turn without allowing the car to drift into adjacent lanes.

Local Traffic Laws and Right Turns:

In California and many other states, it is permissible to make a right turn at a red light, as long as you first come to a complete stop, yielding to pedestrians in the crosswalk and any approaching traffic. If you plan a road trip to other states, be aware that rules may prohibit right turns at red lights.

Sometimes, as you approach an intersection to make a right turn, you will encounter a motorist who has stopped for a red light and failed to properly position their vehicle close enough to the left white line. When such a situation prevents you from making a right turn, the best course of action is to be patient until the other driver moves forward.

Making Left Turns at Typical Traffic Signals

The left turn is one of the most dangerous driving maneuvers.

A left turn at a standard green traffic signal is referred to as an "<u>unprotected</u>," left turn because oncoming traffic has the right-of-way. Improper action can result in a broadside collision, which often causes major injuries and vehicle damage.

As you approach a green traffic signal, first get into the proper left lane to negotiate the left turn. Next, do a traffic check; be sure the left turn is clear, with no vehicles approaching and no pedestrians crossing.

If you observe oncoming traffic that is close enough to be a hazard, you will need to identify the proper position to stop in the intersection. Usually, the correct position is one traffic lane -- or the width of a car -- before the marked concrete divider or double yellow lines. Or, if you're on a residential street, this will be an imaginary line. Stop and wait here until all traffic has passed.

When in doubt, wait. Remember that the yellow light does not give us the right to go first. Again, the oncoming motorists might want to step on the accelerator in an attempt to beat the red light. When this happens, you will be facing a red light. This can be unnerving. Proceed through the turn when your path is clear. Cross traffic should allow you to complete the left turn before they proceed on the green light, because you were legally in the intersection, obeying the unprotected left turn require-ments.

In addition to not obeying the right-of-way rule, other common left-turn mistakes are as follows:

1. Not entering the intersection and positioning your vehicle properly, which will prohibit others from entering the intersection. If you do not reach the proper position, it will also take more time to complete the turn.
2. Positioning your car *too* far into the intersection, thereby interfering with vehicles trying to make a left turn from the opposite direction.
3. Not keeping the wheel straight as you wait for the

green light. If the motorist behind you were to rear-end your car, the impact would force your vehicle into the oncoming traffic.

Making Left Turns That Are Protected

Do not assume that just because you have a green arrow signal, your turn is protected; before you proceed, confirm that oncoming vehicles will yield to you.

A Protected left turn means that you (usually) have the right of way, under one of these conditions:

1. A green arrow signal;
2. A "3-way signal" sign;
3. A "4-way signal" sign; or
4. When two lanes are marked for left turns.

Even when you have the right of way, you need to make

a visual check to verify that other motorists are going to allow you to safely complete the left turn. After positioning in the left lane, you must determine where you want to start the turn, and where you want to complete it.

Normally, you will want to enter the intersection and start the turn at a point that is the width of one lane before the concrete divider or double yellow lines in the street you are moving toward.

On a residential street, begin the left turn approximately one car width before the imaginary line on the cross street. Just like when you make a right turn, find the proper speed for the sharpness of the turn, and then move the wheel accordingly.

As you start the left turn, aim for where you want to complete it. Normally, you want to finish next to the concrete divider, double yellow lines or next to the imaginary line on a residential street. Again, brake and gas coordination as you roll through the turn is very important.

Disobeying Official Stop and Yield Signs

The Stop Sign vs. the Yield Sign: There is a difference!

Stop signs require all motorists – and bicyclists - to come to a complete stop.

I have encountered many motorists and student drivers who have questioned me when I corrected them about making a complete stop.

"I *did* stop," they protest.

Sometimes they were surprised to learn that, no, they did *not* stop. No stop is complete unless all four wheels stop completely.

Often, rolling stops are called "California rolls" or "Hollywood stops." Drivers who are in the habit of doing rolling stops feel that they have slowed down enough to proceed safely across the intersection. To correct this behavior, I teach my students to stop completely, and then count "one thousand one, one thousand two," as they scan for cross traffic, before entering the intersection.

Yield signs are less restrictive than stop signs. They inform you that you must let other traffic go first. As mentioned above, the proper procedure for when you encounter a yield sign is to first be mentally prepared to stop: slow down to 15 miles per hour or slower, adequately check cross traffic, and then, if the way is clear, proceed. If it is not clear, we must yield.

Disobeying Official Traffic Signals

Most motorists disobey regular traffic signals because they are indecisive as to whether to stop or proceed across an intersection after the light has turned yellow. While they are thinking, they are braking, and they reach a point of no return. If they decide to stop at this point, they will end up in the intersection. If they decide to cross, they will eventually run the red light.

To avoid this predicament, I suggest the following technique, which has helped to reform many red-light runners:

Note that the yellow traffic light usually stays on for approximately three seconds. When a road is rated for higher speeds, yellow lights are programmed to be displayed a little longer, mainly because drivers need more time to react – the stopping distance is increased.

When the green light changes to yellow, start counting: "one thousand one, one thousand two." If it takes less than one second for the front of your vehicle to reach the white limit line or the first line of the crosswalk, check for cross traffic, and then proceed carefully across the intersection.

If it takes you one second or more to reach the limit line or first line of the crosswalk, prepare to stop.

The only exception to this guideline is when you observe a tailgater behind you. In this situation, it would probably be a better decision to safely cross with the yellow light than to catch the tailgater off guard and risk a rear-end collision.

Also keep in mind that some motorists believe that the yellow light means "Step on it, you might make it!"

To avoid the serious consequences from this behavior, "traffic checks" (proper scanning) are important.

Seasoned traffic officers will ask drivers involved in collisions at intersections the following question: "Where was the other vehicle when you first observed him / her?" The most common answers are: "I never saw him / her" or "I didn't notice him / her until he / she hit me."

In order to stay safe, we cannot stare ahead or have

tunnel vision. When we do so, we let our guard down, so that we are not ready for the unexpected.

Understanding Intersections and Controls

"T-Bone" traffic collisions usually occur at four-way intersections.

| **4 Way** | *T* | *T – Right* | *T - Left* |

This takes me to one of my favorite exercises, "Reading Intersections."

The configuration of an intersection reveals which

directions other traffic could be approaching us. After we identify what type of intersection we are approaching, we need to focus on the controls at the intersection, if any. In California, if there is an intersection with no controls, the law states that the first motorist that reaches the intersection has the right–of–way; After that, the second car goes second, and so on. I call this the sequence of arrival.

The most dangerous intersections are the ones with *no* stop signs, *only one* stop sign or *two* stop signs. We need to use more caution when crossing or entering these intersections.

When you approach an uncontrolled T-intersection, the traffic on the top of the T has the right of way. Treat this situation as if you have a yield sign. Slow down to 15 miles per hour, or slower, to allow traffic to pass. Proceed when the road is clear.

At T-left and T-right intersections, you have the right of way. Still, you must do a traffic check to ensure that other motorists acknowledge your intention to cross the intersection.

At an intersection where you see only one or two stop signs, stop completely behind the white limit line or the first line of the crosswalk. If you cannot see cross traffic clearly, slowly roll forward to get a better view. This will help you make a better decision as to when to proceed across. Many drivers stop on the limit line, or in the crosswalk, because they are unable to see cross traffic.

When you arrive at a four-way intersection with a stop sign, normally there will be another stop sign across the street to control oncoming traffic in the opposite direction.

The safest intersections are those with three or four stop signs. We stop and proceed according to our sequence of arrival.

When approaching safe intersections, we need to be assertive and follow that sequence of arrival. Otherwise, we confuse other motorists.

There are situations when the other motorist won't allow you the right of way. When this happens, just relinquish the right of way; it is your responsibility to do everything possible to avoid collisions. This includes being aware when another motorist is not going to obey the rules.

Avoiding Rear-End Traffic Collisions

When a motorist collides with the rear end of the car in front of them, they are usually either *following too close or travelling too fast for the conditions.* Under ideal conditions, the guideline is to allow yourself one car length for every 10 miles per hour. During inclement weather, the distance needs to be extended.

Another thing to remember is the "3-Second Rule" rule: When the vehicle in front of you passes a landmark, count "one thousand one, one thousand two, one thousand three." If you reach the same landmark at "one thousand three" or more, you are maintaining a safe following distance. If you arrive before three seconds has elapsed, you are too close, and need to slow down and leave more room.

Any time you're in a position where you couldn't stop in time to avoid a collision, your instincts should alert you to take immediate corrective action, by backing off to obtain the safe distance.

Following too closely, coupled with inattention, causes many multiple-car traffic collisions.

TEN

Effective Freeway Driving

Many people fear freeway driving because of the high speeds involved. It is my opinion that freeway driving is safer than driving on surface streets.

For one thing, freeways have restricted access, so that you can only get on using the on-ramps, and only get off at the off-ramps.

Also, most freeways have structural guards that are designed to prevent head-on traffic collisions. Some examples of these are various types of guard rails or Jersey walls. Freeways do not have intersections; there is no need for us to monitor traffic signals, stop signs, yield signs and similar controls that dictate the right of way.

Traffic engineers have devoted many years toward making our freeways safer. Have you noticed that most stationary structures on freeways have protective barriers, such as sand-filled barrels at major junctions, or steel guard railings in front of light posts and under crossings?

The best benefit of using freeways is that they allow us to get to our destination quicker, and with minimal potential hazards.

 VS.

Many motorists do not understand the difference between these two traffic signs. The left sign depicts a merging situation which requires cooperation and courtesy to blend into one traffic lane. The right sign is intended to show drivers that there is an added lane ahead -- nevertheless, be alert! Confused motorists may attempt to make sudden unnecessary lane changes.

In my experience, the hardest maneuver with freeway driving is actually getting onto the freeway. I suggest the following steps for merging safely on the freeway:

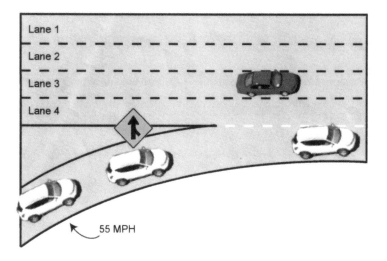

1. The most important task is to accelerate to approximately 55 miles per hour. I recommend this speed because the normal flow of traffic in the slow (# 4) lane usually travels at 55 under normal conditions. Many times, when traffic is congested, we will need to reduce our merging speed to match the flow of

traffic in the slow lane.

2. Turn on the left turn signal when you see the "Merging" sign. This is very important to do at night, because it attracts the attention of motorists traveling in the slow lane; it gives them more time to decide if they are going to be courteous, and allow you to merge safely in front of them.

3. As you are accelerating onto the ramp, monitor your inside and left-side mirrors to check traffic in the slow lane.

4. Normally, on-ramps have a solid white line followed by a broken white line. When you reach the end of the broken white line, occupy the entire width of the ramp.

5. Look over your left shoulder to check traffic in the # 3 lane. In the diagram above, we are looking at the red vehicle in the # 3 lane. We want to make sure that he doesn't attempt to change into the # 4 lane at the same time we attempt to merge into the # 4 lane.

6. Merge safely into the # 4 lane, when it is clear.

7. Cancel your turn signal.

These are the most common errors when merging on the freeway:

1. Merging too slowly or too fast. Merging too slowly will affect the flow of traffic in the # 4 lane – everyone will need to apply their brakes to let you in. Merging too fast will create a hazardous situation; it could

possibly cause other motorists to overreact.

2. Not using the entire ramp.
3. Attempting to enter traffic too early and too slowly.
4. Not looking over your left shoulder at the end of the broken white line to check traffic in the # 3 lane. Do not rely on your mirrors only.

Sometimes students ask me "What do you do when drivers in the # 4 lane don't let you in?" If you have reached a high speed (approximately 55 mph), I suggest using the right emergency shoulder, and then moving onto the freeway when the lane is clear.

In this situation, we place ourselves in a hazardous situation if we slam on the brakes. The chances of getting rear-ended are great, because the person behind might be concentrating on merging and not expecting you to come to a complete stop on the ramp. Remember, use any option to avoid a traffic collision.

When merging onto the freeway at slower speeds during commute traffic, it will be reasonably safe to stop on the ramp if traffic in the slow lane doesn't let you in.

When entering the freeway during times of heavy commute traffic, drivers should take turns, a practice called "Equal Feed." One car in the slow lane passes the on-ramp, then one car from the on-ramp merges into traffic. Using this practice displays courtesy and avoids confusion.

Have you seen metered lights on the on-ramps during commute traffic hours? They are designed to handle the maximum number of vehicles on the freeway systems. It's like pouring water into a funnel. A controlled amount of water will flow smoothly. If we speed up the process, we experience overflow, and random starting and stopping.

Diamond lanes or carpool lanes is another method for alleviating traffic congestion. Its initial purpose was to encourage drivers to share vehicles and reduce the number of vehicles on the freeways. It doesn't make sense to have a solo driver in most vehicles; it is better for the environment to have fewer cars on the road.

Let me share with you a few encounters I experienced patrolling the diamond lanes on my motorcycle in East Los Angeles, California.

The regulations stated that you could use the diamond lanes if you had three or more occupants in the vehicle. My mobility on my motorcycle allowed me to maneuver closer to the diamond lane to monitor the number of occupants in vehicles. On a few occasions, I noticed that the backseat occupants were sitting very still. I moved closer, to see whether they were sleeping. When I took a second look, I was surprised to discover that there was a mannequin strapped in the seat belt, or a doll secured in a baby seat!

On one occasion, I was approaching a vehicle that

seemed to have two occupants in the front seats. However, when I was approximately one car length back, I noticed someone in the rear of the vehicle wave to me. I reciprocated by waving back. As I passed the vehicle, I noticed a black box in the rear seat with an extended shaft and a white glove attached to it. I backed off to make an enforcement stop, guiding the violator to the right shoulder.

After the right front passenger rolled down the window, I noticed an electrical cord leading to the front seat. The driver pushed the button and the arm would wave. The driver accepted his citation. He told me that the device had been saving him forty minutes of commute time every day!

ELEVEN

It is Imperative to Incorporate Defensive Driving Techniques

In 1952, Harold Smith, a traffic safety educator, introduced a method to effectively reduce traffic collisions called "The Smith System," which specifically stressed the importance of space for the car and visibility for the driver.

These are the five keys to the Smith System:

1. **Aim High in Steering** - Aim for the center of your lane far ahead. The farther we see ahead, the quicker we will be able to identify hazardous situations and traffic rules. This gives us more time and distance to react.

    Many drivers wander too much within their traffic lane. Looking further ahead is an instant cure. Any time you are looking down over the hood of the car, you will find yourself moving the wheel too much.

    We have a tendency to drive in the direction that we are looking. If you are aiming high in steering, your mind should communicate with your hands to stay still on the wheel and avoid unnecessary movement.

    As you negotiate curves in the roadway, it is important to look toward the area where you are headed. When the road curves to the left, guide your vehicle along the white broken traffic line, double yellow lines or the concrete island on the left side of your lane. When you are negotiating a curve to the right, your target area would be on the right broken traffic line, right edge of the traffic lane or on the solid white line separating the emergency lane on the freeway.

A common driver error is not looking at a point far enough ahead of the curve, resulting in over-steering. Again, it is very important to aim high in steering. Once you move the wheel to negotiate the curve, hold that position and let the car do the work. Also, while you are driving through the curve, keep lifting your eyes toward the target area ahead, to guide your vehicle. I call this technique the "moving target."

2. **See the Big Picture** – Look not just at the street, but at both side areas as well, about one block ahead.

   Imagine the traffic picture as a puzzle. All participants and objects are individual pieces. We are looking for other motorists, pedestrians, bicycles, motorcycles, skateboarders, and animals, plus considering the road and weather conditions. Failure to identify one piece of the puzzle will create an incomplete picture – and an incomplete picture presents a potential hazard.

3. **Keep Your Eyes Moving** - Scan ahead and to the sides. Check your mirrors approximately every six or seven seconds to keep yourself alert. This

practice will prevent tunnel vision, which limits the effectiveness of your peripheral vision. This will also help you anticipate unexpected surprises, such as motorcyclists maneuvering between traffic lanes.

4. **Make Sure They See You** - Warn others of your intentions by signaling and placing your vehicle in the proper position on the roadway. I call this "jockeying for position." We need to stay out of other motorists' blind spots. Sometimes we have to position our vehicle in front of others or drop back so that the other drivers can see us in their rearview mirrors.

5. **Leave Yourself an Out** - Have an alternative safe path for your car if you need to take evasive action. For example, avoid passing in the extreme right lane on a bridge where there is no right shoulder. If another driver were to attempt to change lanes at that location, you would have no place to go. Again, jockeying for position allows you to maintain a safe cushion of space around your vehicle.

TWELVE

Making Good Driving Decisions

What is the first decision you need to make before getting behind the wheel? You are correct if you thought about whether you were sober enough to drive. The experience I gained as an educator and former state traffic officer gave me a very clear understanding of the consequences people face when arrested for, and convicted of, driving under the influence.

You are responsible for your own decisions and actions. Many arrestees are remorseful for the pain and suffering they cause innocent motorists. They acknowledge the fact that saying "I'm sorry" doesn't rectify the situation. If your sobriety is in question, don't take any chances.

Law-enforcement agencies are doing a good job keeping DUI collisions to a minimum by using the following tools and innovations:

- DUI Checkpoints

- Federal grants
- Officers that are well-trained in recognizing signs of drug use
- Cell-phone communications systems that allow other drivers to report DUIs by dialing 911
- Community organizations that demand action, including Mothers Against Drunk Driving (MADD) and Students Against Drunk Driving (SADD)
- Ride-hailing companies
- High costs for DUI convictions. A drunk driver -- even one who is not involved in a collision -- will still be looking at paying approximately $10,000. That includes attorneys' fees, court costs and fines, towing fees, and DUI first offenders' course fees.

Earlier, I discussed the different types of people who disobey traffic laws. While laws are necessary to reduce conflicts that result in traffic collisions, a conscientious driver obeying all the traffic laws will *still* be vulnerable in traffic if he or she does not make good defensive driving decisions.

Let's review the I.P.D.E process, which stands for "Identify, Predict, Decide, Execute." This system helps us to stay focused on handling different traffic situations. It should be a part of the curriculum in modern driver education classes.

Identify – This step refines visual search techniques.

We are looking for potential hazards ahead. For example, in approaching intersections, we must do traffic checks (scanning) before we cross. Even though we have the right of way, we must be sure that other drivers won't run the red light, stop sign or yield sign. When we recognize the potential hazards in advance, we are able to focus on the next step.

Predict - We need to predict what the other party will do. Will the pedestrian step off the curb at the last moment? Will the unleashed dog dart in front of your vehicle? Will the tailgater continue to get closer behind your vehicle?

Decide -Next, you need to decide what plan of action is necessary. Be decisive about your ability to control the situation. Sometimes indecision will get us in trouble. It is imperative to make safe decisions. Avoid taking chances. Do not attempt to beat a yellow traffic signal. Waiting at a red signal light for a few seconds will take you less time than exchanging information for a traffic collision report!

Execute - Follow through with the correct plan of action. Many times, when you clearly demonstrate your intentions, you assist others in making decisions. In California, a good example is when there are four stop signs, and you arrive first. After stopping, you should expect to go first – but also look to be sure that the other drivers will allow you to proceed.

Let me share with you a real situation that illustrates the importance of making the right defensive driving decision.

Several years ago, I was patrolling the Pomona Freeway in Los Angeles when I received a call. It was a traffic collision, with no details known. When I arrived at the scene, I noticed cars parked on the emergency shoulder. A vehicle was over the embankment, resting on its roof. A female driver had sustained major injuries and was trapped in the driver's seat.

After the ambulance, fire department and tow truck were summoned, the first responders used a tool called the Jaws of Life to extricate the driver.

At the conclusion of my investigation, I determined the actual sequence of events that occurred.

The trouble started with a dog running on the emergency shoulder of the eastbound freeway. The driver was following her fiancé in the slow (#4) lane of the freeway, going approximately 55 mph. As the fiancé was passing the dog, he sounded his horn. This startled the dog; he darted between the two vehicles. The bride-to-be swerved to her right to avoid hitting the dog. She lost control of her vehicle and ran off the embankment. This caused her vehicle to flip over several times.

Unfortunately, the young woman ended up paralyzed from the waist down.

Was it justified for her fiancé to sound the horn?
Was it necessary for her to swerve to avoid the dog?
The answer to both questions is "No."

Most of the time, when you are confronted with animals on the roadway, your best plan of action is to *brake only*. When we swerve for animals, we usually make the situation worse. If we swerve to the left, we could be going into oncoming traffic. By swerving to the right, we could strike a stationary object or go off the embankment, as in the case of the young lady.

The same principle applies when you encounter opened doors in the roadway. Do not respond instantly by swerving into the adjacent lane to avoid the door. There is no reason to involve a third party, such as another car or motorcycle that you do not see in the lane. The best action to take is to *brake only*. If necessary, come to a complete stop until the driver closes the door. Maintain control of the situation, avoiding swerving for open doors.

THIRTEEN

The Driver's Test Experience

As we all know, the key element of passing any test is being prepared. I have met many students who have taken the drive test multiple times before coming to me. Most of them weren't prepared. They were learning about their deficiencies each time they failed.

Driving examiners have an important job: it is up to them to determine which applicants will be allowed to operate a motor vehicle on our highway system.

If the examiners have any reservations concerning one's ability to operate a vehicle safely, they are responsible for determining if you have failed the test. This means you will need to return when you can demonstrate the following basic skills:

1. Your ability to control the vehicle,
2. Your ability to obey all traffic laws, and
3. Whether you can handle any potential hazards that might arise during the drive test.

Part of passing the test is demonstrating your ability to make sound driving decisions.

Either taking the driver's test for the first time or being re-tested behind the wheel can be a very trying experience.

There used to be a certain driving examiner at one Department of Motor Vehicles office who was tagged in internet postings as "Scary Larry." He gained that reputation because he was extremely strict with teenage driver applicants.

I grew to like Larry. He was sincere in his efforts to ensure that the novice drivers he examined would be safe on the road. He reminded me of a quality-control engineer, making sure that all the moving parts – people driving on our roadways - will perform properly. That is the way to maintain the smooth operation of our overall highway system. I considered Larry a valuable member of my team. We were unified in our efforts to eliminate unnecessary injuries and deaths.

California driving examiners need to be brave: they must test applicants in vehicles that do not have dual brakes.

As you prepare for the test, keep in mind that the examiner would prefer for you to pass. If you fail, the examiner knows that you will have to re-schedule. Many DMV offices are shorthanded; they don't need the extra workload!

In California, drive test applicants are required to be accompanied by a licensed driver who is at least 18 years old. If applicant is a minor, the licensed driver must be 25 years or older.

Try to arrive at your scheduled test approximately

15 minutes early. Most DMV offices will require you to re-schedule if you are late. You must bring your instruction permit, current vehicle registration and proof of insurance. Applicants who are under 18 years of age must also present driver training certificates.

Prior to positioning your vehicle for the drive test, make sure your seat, steering wheel and mirrors are adjusted. Your seat belt should also be fastened.

When the examiner approaches your vehicle, roll down the window and greet him or her with a friendly smile. This demonstrates your confidence and makes a good initial impression. After you have read the statement explaining the scoring procedure for the test, the examiner will ask for your signature. Next, the examiner will ask you to turn the ignition switch to the "on" position, without starting the engine.

The examiner will ask you to point out various controls that might be necessary during the drive test:

- Parking / emergency brake
- Front window defroster
- Windshield wipers
- Emergency / hazard lights
- Headlights

Normally, examiners will not have you activate the

controls unless they will be needed during the test.

After the examiner inspects the vehicle by walking around it in a circle, he or she will sit in the right front seat. At this time, there are two things you should do:

1. Roll up the window so that you can hear the examiner's commands better, and
2. Turn the ignition to the "off" position so that you don't wear down the battery.

The examiner realizes that some applicants will feel nervous or uneasy during the drive test. Try to relax. Imagine that the examiner is your parent, driving instructor or other person who helped you prepare for the test. Often, applicants try so hard that they fail to stay focused on their driving responsibilities.

Only give the examiner what he / she requests. Just because they ask you to change lanes to the left, that doesn't mean that the examiner wants you to make a left turn at the corner. Don't react to the examiner's command too quickly. If you do, you are more likely to momentarily confuse left and right. This could result in errors such as turning right when you have been asked to make a left turn. One trick for avoiding this is to think "signal up" for a right turn and "signal down" for a left turn.

Drive tests in other states, provinces or countries may be

a little different. However, their main objective is the same: to provide licenses to applicants who demonstrate safe driving practices.

Critical Driving Errors - In California, any critical "driving error" is an automatic disqualification:

1. **Intervention by Driving Examiner** –
    - ✓ Any physical or verbal intervention being required during the test.
    - ✓ The necessity for the examiner to grab the steering wheel or apply the emergency brake.
    - ✓ The examiner having to instruct you to stop for a pedestrian, traffic sign, signal or other impending hazard situation.

2. **Striking an Object or a Curb** -
    - ✓ Striking a pedestrian, animal or object in the roadway that could have been safely avoided.
    - ✓ Striking the right curb while negotiating a right turn.
    - ✓ Striking the right curb while parking or during the "backing straight and slow" exercise.

3. **Disobeying Traffic Signs or Signal** –
    - ✓ Disobeying stop or yield signs.
    - ✓ Disobeying a "keep clear" sign.
    - ✓ Disregarding a sign that indicates "Fewer Lanes Ahead."
    - ✓ Failure to proceed with a green traffic light.

- ✓ Failure to stop at a red light, flashing red light, or red arrow signal.
- ✓ Disobeying painted arrows or curb markings, or improperly navigating a traffic island.
- ✓ Making a turn despite a "No Turn On Red" sign.

4. Disobeying Traffic Personnel or Safety Vehicles –
- ✓ Failure to pull over to the right and stop for an emergency vehicle.
  Here is the correct procedure to follow when an emergency vehicle approaches: If you are in an intersection, safely cross it. Then pull to the right and stop. You do not want to obstruct the intersection, especially when an emergency vehicle is approaching. You do not know which route the emergency vehicle will take.
- ✓ Failure to obey safety personnel, law enforcement officers or firefighters directing traffic.
- ✓ Failure to stop for a school bus with flashing red lights.

5. Making a Dangerous Maneuver - You Will Fail If You:
- ✓ Execute any action, or fail to take a necessary action, that results in another driver or pedestrian being required to take evasive action.
- ✓ Violate another motorist's or pedestrian's right of way.
- ✓ Fail to check traffic at any intersection when a potential hazard is present.

✓ Make any unnecessary stop that interferes with traffic.
✓ Enter an intersection when there isn't ample room to clear it.
✓ Do not look over your shoulder prior to making a lateral movement (a lane change, merging into traffic, pulling to the curb or to the side of the road).

6. Speed – You Will Fail If You:
✓ Drive 10 mph over the posted speed limit.
✓ Drive 10 mph under the speed limit, impeding the normal flow of traffic.
✓ Drive at an unsafe speed during inclement weather or despite adverse road conditions. This principle is known as the "Basic Speed Law."

7. Auxiliary Equipment Use – You Will Fail If You:
✓ Don't use your windshield wipers, headlights or defroster during inclement weather.
✓ Don't use your headlights after dark.
✓ Don't sound your horn when a vehicle in front is backing unsafely.

8. Lane Violation– You Will Fail If You:
✓ Don't stay in your lane.
✓ Drive more than 200 feet in a bike lane or a two-way center left turn lane.
✓ Do not obey designated turn lanes.
✓ Make a turn from a wrong lane.

- ✓ Don't look over your shoulder prior to changing lanes.
- ✓ Look over your shoulder and change lanes at the same time.
- ✓ Interfere with other motorists while executing a lane change.

FOURTEEN

Re-evaluation of Senior Drivers

Very soon, 40 percent of the population will be over 55 years of age.

On several occasions, my senior students have let me know from the outset that they have been driving for over 40 years without being involved in a traffic collision. They have also mentioned that the DMV was focusing on them only because of their age.

The DMV has a responsibility to monitor all drivers for their own safety and for the safety of the public. The news media seems to focus on traffic collisions involving seniors. One of the most popular themes is called "Pedal Confusion Syndrome." Pedal application errors occur frequently, all across the country. The National Highway Traffic Safety Administration states that "Pedal error accidents occur up to 16,000 times every year in the United States. That means there are approximately 44 pedal error accidents on any given day."[8]

A senior driver inadvertently steps on the gas instead of the brake and then drives into a building, causing injuries. This kind of incident, often highly publicized, always places pressure on the DMV to do something to correct the problem. But I truly believe that that DMV officials want to allow seniors to retain their driving privilege, *as long as* they

---

8   Willoughby Brod, LLP "The All-Too Common Tie Between Pedal Confusion and Storefront Crashes" https://www.sanfranciscoinjurylawyerblog.com/common-tie-pedal-confusion-storefront-crashes/ (accessed 6/3/2019).

can demonstrate their ability to drive safely.

Many seniors do not want to abandon their ability to get behind the wheel and enjoy the freedom to transport themselves. My senior students have expressed to me their fear that losing their driving privilege would put an end to their independence. They don't want to inconvenience family members and friends. Some seniors view losing their license as if it were a death sentence.

There is only one California driving regulation specifically targeting seniors: after age 70, motorists must renew their license every five years in person, rather than by mail. For those appointments, drivers are given a vision and written test. No road test is given unless a DMV employee deems it necessary.

According to the Governors Highway Safety Association, mature drivers most often face impairments to their vision (reduced contrast sensitivity and increased time needed to adjust to changes in light levels); cognitive abilities (memory, visual processing, attention and executive skills); and motor functions (muscle strength, endurance and flexibility).[9]

The Insurance Institute for Highway Safety says fatal

---

9   Governors Highway Safety Association, "Mature Drivers," September 26, 2011. https://www.ghsa.org/issues/mature-drivers (accessed 6/3/2019).

crash rates per mile traveled increase after age 75, and they increase notably after age 80. This isn't, however, largely due to an increased tendency to get into crashes. It's often due to medical issues that older drivers have while they are behind the wheel.

Some indications that seniors are not doing their best behind the wheel:

- Minor fender benders,
- Traffic citations, and
- Trouble remembering directions to once-familiar locations.

Let me share an incident that happened to one of my students. Marie took her puppy to the veterinarian in a town where she had lived for over 15 years. She was unable to locate her vehicle afterward, so she called the police. The officer got a description of her vehicle and located it a block away. Later, Marie received a notice that she had to report to the DMV for re-examination. She had to demonstrate her cognitive skills in a drive test.

Here's another incident: While on patrol in the right lane of a freeway in Los Angeles, I noticed a vehicle attempting to merge on the freeway at approximately 35 mph, while the flow of traffic was 62 mph.

This driver's maneuver caused a big rig hauling two

trailers to fishtail in two adjacent lanes, which in turn caused traffic to come to a halt. I passed the scene on the right shoulder and made an enforcement stop. I escorted the senior driver off the freeway, gave him directions on how to reach his destination on the surface streets and submitted a form to the Department of Motor Vehicles to have this driver's abilities re-evaluated.

There is no set age when a person's keys should be taken away. Aging does not guarantee that a driver's abilities will decline.

There are many things people can do to prolong their time on the road:

Have your vision and hearing checked routinely. The removal of cataracts and updating your eyeglass prescription can significantly improve your vision.

Get plenty of rest before attempting to drive beyond your familiar surroundings. Dozing off behind the wheel can compromise the safety of drivers, their passengers and fellow motorists.

Know your medications; be familiar with the manufacturer's directions and restrictions, especially warnings that state "Do not operate vehicles or machinery." They're warning you that this medication can make you drowsy.

Recognize your limitations. Driving at night and during inclement weather can be challenging. If you feel uncomfortable during these conditions, confine your driving to more favorable conditions.

Enroll in a refresher course. Reputable driving schools have qualified instructors to assist you in correcting any critical driving errors. This support will build your confidence.

On occasion, family members call me to request a driving evaluation for a senior. A second opinion from a reputable driving instructor can help determine if an older person is still capable of handling their driving responsibilities.

I clearly remember my experience with a student named Tom. He informed me from the outset when he drove by himself, he committed no driving errors. During our lesson, he attempted to run two stop signs and a red light!

After our short driving assessment, we returned to his residence. There, I informed his family that it was my professional opinion that Tom needed to seek other means of transportation in the interest of his own safety and that of the general public. Sometimes it is difficult to break bad driving habits.

Another student, Eugene, contacted me to assist him

in preparing for his behind the wheel drive test. He was adamant that he didn't need to look over his shoulder before changing lanes. He felt the use of his mirrors were adequate to change lanes safely. I informed him that the DMV examiner would fail him for committing this critical driving error. Since he didn't believe me, I asked Eugene to ask the examiner what would happen if he didn't look over his shoulder prior to changing lanes. Of course, the examiner told him that this critical error would cause him to fail. He would then have to return for another drive test, to demonstrate that he checked the blind spots adequately.

On many occasions, I advise my senior students that the best person to decide whether to stop driving is *yourself*. An aging person knows their own capabilities and how they feel behind the wheel. They are aware when their vision is deficient, whether their cognitive skills are satisfactory and whether they are comfortable in handling hazardous situations.

Helpful Technology for Senior Drivers

The automobile industry has provided many helpful, innovative features that can aid senior drivers:

Push Button Entry / Start Controls - Benefits drivers who suffer from arthritic hands, painful or stiff fingers or diminished fine motor skills. The remote push-button entry / start feature eliminates ever having to twist a key, as long as an encoded key fob is on one's pocket or purse.

Extendable Sun Visors - Can be very helpful to motorists who have vision problems, especially those with slow recovery from excessive brightness and glare.

Heated Seats and Steering Wheel - Can help ease stiff joints or lower back pain while in route. This is helpful even in warmer climates.

Digital Speedometer - Seniors with vision problems should look for vehicles with large digital speedometers that can be easier to see and process at a glance than a conventional gauge.

Tilt /Telescopic Steering Wheels and Power Adjustable Brake/Accelerator Pedals - help drivers of all sizes find the optimal "fit."

Parking Aids - Such as a rearview camera and / or proximity warning can help drivers with diminished upper-body range of motion. These features allow drivers to minimize twisting and upper-body rotation during the process of backing out of a garage or parking space.

Adaptive Cruise Control - This high-tech enhancement of familiar automotive technology enables a car to maintain both a set speed and a safe distance from the traffic ahead. The system slows the car down and speeds it up automatically as needed. Some cruise control systems are even able to operate in stop-and go traffic.

Blind Spot Warning - Sensors or cameras alert a driver to the presence of other cars to the side and rear of the vehicle. This is very helpful on the highway, where the driver might not otherwise be able to locate other vehicles in the blind spots. Many such systems can also issue an alert if there is cross traffic approaching during the process of backing out of a garage or parking space.

It's important to note that even with these technical aids, California and other states still require motorists to look over their shoulder prior to changing lanes or making other lateral maneuvers.

Navigation Systems – No one wants to get lost. Having a GPS (Global Positioning System) can be especially helpful to those having problems reading street signs while driving. Spoken information from the GPS allows drivers to concentrate on the road instead of diverting their attention to a display screen. For safety, it is important to pay more attention to freeway signs than to the details of navigation. It is also important to avoid last minute decisions that result in abrupt turns.

Automatic Day / Night Mirrors - If you are having problems seeing clearly while driving at night, these auto-dimming interior and side mirrors will help minimize glare after sunset.

FIFTEEN

How Autonomous Vehicles Could Influence the Traffic Collision Picture

In 2015, the website ScienceAlert.com announced, "A new report has analyzed the impact of driverless cars on the incidence of fatal traffic accidents, and say that simply by taking human emotions and errors out of the equation, we could reduce deaths on the road by 90 percent. That's almost 300,000 lives saved each decade in the US, and a saving of $190 billion each year in healthcare costs associated with accidents."[10] Ideally, autonomous vehicles could impact the lives of millions.

If implemented as effectively as designers hope, these vehicles will make driving safer for older drivers, and easier for everyone. The vehicles will be controlled through a combination of sensors, lasers, cameras, software and intricate maps.

I can appreciate the fact that the technology is focused on correcting driver error – the cause of most crashes. The elimination of distracted driving is a major selling point for the technology.

Sophisticated Lidar™ systems allow autonomous vehicles to "see" the road. Lasers bounce invisible beams of light off objects, then gauge the distance by measuring how long it takes for the beam to bounce back. Knitting millions of these signals together creates images called "point clouds."

---

10   Science Alert, "Driverless Cars Could Reduce Traffic Fatalities by Up to 90%, Says Report," October 1, 2015. https://www.sciencealert.com/driverless-cars-could-re-duce-traffic-fatalities-by-up-to-90-says-report (accessed 6/3/2019).

This paints a picture of the world around the car.

The technology will need to identify buildings and traffic signals. It will need to distinguish between people and animals, between bicycles and motorcycles and between rocks and soccer balls, according to their shape and the direction in which they are moving.

Features of Autonomous Vehicles

Adaptive Cruise Control - uses forward-looking sensors to maintain both a vehicle's set speed and a safe following distance from the traffic ahead. This can be especially helpful to drivers with diminished reflexes.

Forward Collision Warning / Prevention System - uses radar, cameras or lasers to monitor the distance between a vehicle and the traffic or other obstruction in its path. The system warns the driver if the vehicle is closing in too fast on another car or other obstruction. Some systems will apply the brakes at full force if the driver isn't reacting quickly enough. Other systems are designed to work at slower speeds in city traffic or in reverse gear. These features are especially helpful to drivers having reduced reaction times.

Lane Departure System - is designed to signal an alert when a vehicle on the highway inadvertently wanders into another lane. Advanced systems will detect when a car has drifted across lane markers, then use steering and/ or braking to help "nudge" a wandering car back into the center of the lane.

Bad weather may prove to be a major issue for the deployment of self-driving cars. What happens if heavy rain, snow, dense fog, mud or even sandstorms block a radar sensor or blur a camera's lens? Built-in washers and defrosters might help, but they probably won't solve the problem entirely.

What if the cameras can't see highway lane markers or visibility otherwise becomes compromised during a storm? Having new cars that can stop themselves presents the risk of lulling drivers into a false sense of security - and even to sleep!

Another big question: How do you get owners to trust the technology, so they'll actually use it?

At the current state-of-the-art, autonomous vehicle technologies tend to fail when they're around pedestrians, cyclists and human drivers. Industry standards must be established to address various issues. How will robot cars need to respond to flaggers at construction sites? How quickly must they pull over safely and stop in the event of a system failure?

How can autonomous cars be programmed to safely

hand control back to a human driver when the self-driving software and sensors have become overwhelmed or overmatched?

The most vexing engineering problem for autonomous vehicle designers is that human behavior is unpredictable. Programmers must design around human behavior and local traffic idiosyncrasies. Not only do human drivers make "California stops," there's also the "Pittsburgh Left." In some regions – notably Pittsburgh, Pennsylvania -- it is customary to let one oncoming car turn left in front of a lane of traffic after the signal turns green.

On a more positive note: When this technology is fully developed, it promises to compensate for the mistakes every driver makes, simply because the automated systems are always alert. They are always monitoring the road ahead. They never get drowsy, distracted or drunk.

In my opinion, the technology behind autonomous vehicles is by no means ready for prime time. We are still years away from a technology that is safe enough to use in the real world.

SIXTEEN

Conclusion and Final Tune-Up Checklist

Mindfulness is a mental state achieved by focusing on awareness in the present moment. It is all about performing at your peak. It is our responsibility as community members to eliminate the unnecessary collisions that result in property damage, injuries and fatalities. Your commitment to preventing traffic collisions will make a difference in society, so that we move beyond the idea that collisions are inevitable.

The Driver Tune-Up Checklist:

- ☐ My sobriety is the most important factor before I get behind the wheel.
- ☐ I will ensure that all my passengers and I are properly using their seat belts before I start the engine.
- ☐ While I am behind the wheel, I will make driving my *number-one priority*.
- ☐ I will be mindful and use systematic thinking in handling traffic situations: Identify, Predict, Decide and Execute.
- ☐ I will continuously work on improving my driving by monitoring my own performance.
- ☐ I will maintain control of my driving, to ensure that I protect myself, passengers and other users of our highway system.
- ☐ I will drive defensively to avoid giving less careful drivers any opportunity to place my passengers and me in harm's way
- ☐ I understand that the key to defensive driving is to

stay focused on my driving responsibilities.

- [ ] I will strive to do everything possible to prevent traffic collisions.
- [ ] I will extend courtesy to other highway users and acknowledge any courtesy extended to me.
- [ ] I will make rational decisions that will eliminate risky close calls.
- [ ] I will obey traffic laws, including limiting use of cell phones, for the safety of all motorists.
- [ ] I will avoid distractions that are under my control.
- [ ] I will forgive errant drivers, in order to avoid road rage.
- [ ] I will ensure that my vehicle is maintained for safe operation.
- [ ] I understand that it is NOT OK to crash.

You *can* make a difference in eliminating unnecessary traffic collisions occurring on our highways! And with that said, I wish you "Happy Motoring."